Prague

The Golden City

Vitalis

PRAGUE

The Golden City

A book of photographs with texts
by Harald Salfellner

Vitalis

© Vitalis, s.r.o., Praha 2005

Translated from the German original by Monica Sperling
Printed by Finidr, Český Těšín

ISBN 80-7253-219-7
www.vitalisknihy.cz

Contents

The **Castle District** seen from Petřín Hill.

THE CASTLE DISTRICT

The old imperial stronghold (Prague Castle) and the adjoining Castle District [Hradčany] are situated on an elongated rocky hill on the left bank of the River Vltava. The name of the district is derived from the Czech term "hrad" meaning castle. Apart from the extended Castle Courtyards, the Royal Gardens and the Summer Residence "Belvedere", the former suburbs including the impressive Strahov Monastery also belong to this district. The influential gentlemen of the country erected their palaces in this distinguished quarter, in close proximity of the king. The Martinic, Černín, Lobkowicz, Rosenberg, Schwarzenberg and Dietrichstein families lived there at eye-level with his Majesty the Emperor. The building plots in the Castle District became scarce in the 17th century hence the nobility was forced to move towards the foot of the hill, to the Lesser Town [Malá Strana].

The beginnings of the Prague Castle lead back to the 9th century. Emperor Charles IV of Luxembourg made the Castle that had fallen to ruin during the times of Přemysl Otakar II into the focal point of the Holy Roman Empire. This is where the Gothic St Vitus Cathedral was erected in 1344 when the city was elevated to archbishopric.

After several years of decline following the Hussite wars, towards the end of the 15th century the Jagiellonian kings moved back to the Castle with their resplendent life and activity since they deemed it necessary to leave the unsafe royal seat in the city after the rebellions in Prague in 1483.

The Habsburgs (since 1526) surrounded the structure with gardens, built the splendid Summer Residence "Belvedere" and transformed the dreary stronghold into a comfortable Castle.

The fire in 1541 that devastated the Lesser Town and the Castle District left a breach in the medieval character of the town. But at the same time, the necessary construction and reconstruction that followed helped in the final breakthrough of the already proclaimed Renaissance period.

The stronghold underwent a renewed blossoming under Rudolph II, the legendary Emperor who made Prague into the cultural and political focus of the Holy Roman Empire one last time. The collector, patron of arts and builder had a series of architectural extensions built (for example, the north wing with the Spanish Hall and the Rudolph Gallery) and had a deer enclosure installed in the moat behind the Castle, also the stone Lion Courtyard, a pheasantry, a fishpond as well as a summer riding school.

In 1618 the signal for the estates rebellion and Thirty Years' War is believed to have been given from the Prague Castle, the so-called Second Defenestration of Prague. The imperial governors Jaroslav Martinic and Vilém of Slavata along with their secretary Phillipus Fabricius were thrown out from a window of the Bohemian Chancellery.

Had Emperor Rudolph II elevated the complete quarter to royal district thus 150 years later, Maria Theresa declared this "Castle District" as the fourth district of Prague.

In connection with Maria Theresa's wars of succession, the stronghold was damaged several times by besieging armies (a French-Saxon Army in 1741, the Prussians in 1744 and 1757) but also boisterous celebrations in the 18th century: the canonisation of John of Nepomuk (1721), the festivities at the coronation of Charles VI as King of Bohemia (1711) and finally the enthronement of Maria Theresa (1743), the ultimately victorious and acclaimed Empress after bitter battles concerning the succession.

After 1918 the president of the young Czechoslovakian Republic, Tomáš Garrigue Masaryk, held office at the Castle, the seat of the country's governing authority. The entire Prague Castle was reconstructed to suit the requirements of the Presidential Chancellery. In 1920 the Slovene architect Josip Plečnik began remodelling the Castle Gardens and courtyard as well as the president's residence and the representation rooms. The reconstruction and research work carry on even into the present times.

Since 1993, the president of the Czech Republic officiates from the Prague Castle.

In the course of centuries the **Premonstratensian monastery Strahov** developed into one of the most significant religious centres and the richest abbey in the country, into a place of arts and sciences.

The **Loretto Shrine:** The attractive west façade adorned with elaborate relief ornaments by Kilian Ignaz Dientzenhofer with the octagonal belfry originates from the years 1721/22.

Černín Palace (the Ministry of Foreign Affairs): Three entranceways emphasise the symmetry of this imposing palace that dominates the dainty Loretto Square like a potentate's fortress. The Palace Garden is only open to the public for concerts and theatre performances in summer.

The **Capuchin monastery** was the first Capuchin monastery in Bohemia. In the connected Church of Our Dear Lady to the Angels that conforms in its plainness to the order's indigence ideal, is a beautiful statue of St Mary.

In the 16th century, on the northern outskirts of the Castle District, over the trench of the Brusnice stream, emerged a frugal settlement: the **"New World".**

Spring and summer at the **New World**: In all of Bohemia, throughout Europe, actually all over the world, we encounter **St Nepomuk** as a silent guard.

Although the small houses in the little lane were burned down many times in the course of centuries; the district has nevertheless retained its romantic charm. The people living here were certainly not wealthy but they were fortunate to have a roof over their heads. What a wonder that they endorsed their dwellings with the proud attribute "golden"! The picturesque **New World** has, in the meantime, become a distinguished artist's quarter and its tranquillity is a pleasant contrast to the lively bustle of the Golden Lane.

Idyll on the **Castle District**.

View of the **Castle Square** from St Vitus Cathedral.

The **Tuscany Palace** was owned by the Dukes of Tuscany since 1718.

2

1. The **Schwarzenberg Palace** was built by Johann Count Lobkowicz in the Florentine style between 1545 and 1563. An Army Museum was accommodated in this sgraffitoed palace for several years, now the National Gallery has found a home here.

2. Through a wrought-iron gate opposite the Riding School, one arrives in the Royal Gardens. A short distance ahead is the sgraffitoed Royal **Ball Game Hall** built between 1567 and 1569, formerly an open loggia structure by Bonifaz Wolmut.

1 In the beginning, when the first tulips in Central Europe blossomed here, the **Royal Gardens** were a Renaissance paradise. Old vineyards were replaced by greenery by the Emperor Ferdinand I and his successors in the 16th century and now exude the charm of an English Park. **St Vitus Cathedral** in the background.

2 In front of the Palace **"Belvedere"** used as exhibition rooms nowadays, the Singing Fountain cast in 1568 attracts the attention of strollers. This marvellous summer palace was a gift from Emperor Ferdinand I to his wife Anna Jagiello.

Gigant at the Castle Portal.

PRAGUE CASTLE

The so-called Courtyard of Honour can be entered through a wrought-iron gate with the monograms of the Empress Maria Theresa and her son Joseph II, guarded by two regiment guards.

The building wings originate from the second half of the 18th century and mark in their austerity the end of Prague Baroque. At that time, after the Seven Years' War against the Prussians, Empress Maria Theresa entrusted the Viennese architect Nicolo Pacassi with the reconstruction of the Imperial Palace.

The Matthew Gate (1614) is considered the earliest example of Prague Baroque. Emperor Matthew I entrusted the famous Italian master builder Vincenzo Scamozzi with its construction. The Theresian architect had the gate previously belonging to the stronghold complex integrated in the entrance tract. The slim flagpoles flanking the portals make us aware for the first time of the world of shapes of the Slovene architect Josip Plečnik. From the passage to the Second Castle Courtyard, a stately staircase on the right leads to the representation rooms, the erstwhile Imperial Chambers. To the left, a newer staircase leads to one of the porticos designed by Josip Plečnik. From here one can access other stately rooms, for example, the Rothmayer Hall, the Spanish Hall and the Rudolph Gallery. Most of the representation rooms however are not accessible to the public. Only a select few are permitted the viewing of the Throne Hall, the Habsburg-, Brožík-, Mirror-, Music-, Social- or Čermák Salons. The early Baroque sandstone fountain in the Second Courtyard stems from the Prague stonemasons Hieronymus Kohl and the Italian Francesco della Torre. Until 1918, this fountain at the feet of the four Roman gods (Vulcanus, Hercules, Neptune, and Mercury) was crowned by an imperial eagle.

In later years (1961–1990), the treasure of St Vitus Cathedral was stored in the Chapel of the Holy Cross. This late Baroque place of worship was built by Anselmo Lurago who based it on the plans of the court architect Pacassi. In the 19th century the chapel was reconstructed in a classicist manner. The chapel's interior, painted and adorned with biblical motives, especially the crucifixion painting at the altar is worth mentioning.

The Chapel of the Holy Cross was the family chapel of the unfortunate monarch Ferdinand I who, since his abdication in 1848 lived at the Prague Castle in quiet seclusion. On the opposite side is the entrance to the Castle Gallery where significant works from the imperial collections are exhibited (Rubens, Tintoretto, Titian and Veronese, to name a few). The Rudolphine Stables to the north are also utilised for exhibition purposes.

View of **Prague Castle**, in the foreground (left of the centre) the Old Royal Palace. The complicated architectonic construction of the building impressively mirrors the style epochs of the past centuries.

On the southwest corner of the St Vitus Cathedral is the **Old Provosty** of the cathedral chapter, the former seat of the bishops in Prague.

ST VITUS CATHEDRAL

In the 11th century, in place of the Romanesque rotunda, a three nave basilica that would serve the Přemyslid dynasty as the coronation and burial church was constructed. In 1344 Emperor Charles IV entrusted the French architect Matthew of Arras with the construction of the Gothic cathedral. After his death in 1352, the building work was set forth by the Swabian Peter Parler with a substantially altered fundamental conception. The Hussite wars brought the construction to a standstill in 1419. Its completion was to follow only in the 20th century by the cathedral master builders Kamil Hilbert and Josef Mocker in neo-Gothic style. The official opening ceremony of the 124 m long cathedral took place in 1929.

The west front of the cathedral is adorned with statues and is overlooked by two 82 m high neo-Gothic spires. The bishop's church can be entered through three exquisitely detailed portals with relief decorated bronze doors.

It would fill a far more extensive publication if one wanted to describe in detail the art treasures and peculiarities of the various chapels of the St Vitus Cathedral. The most important chapel certainly is the high Gothic St Wenceslas Chapel.

Through the Hasenburg Chapel situated to the south, one arrives at the spiral staircase that leads to the upper tower level and to the bells. The panorama from the top is unique!

It pays not to shy away from a narrow stairwell with 285 stairs solely for this incredible view. On the southern exterior of the cathedral is the impressive large copper topped St Vitus belfry. The Renaissance master builder Bonifaz Wolmut lent it the characteristic roof shape. Behind a lancet window with a gilded ornamental grille hangs, since 1549, the heaviest bell in the country with its 18 tons in weight – the name "Sigismund" was chosen for it.

The crowned "R" above the window reminds of the Habsburg Emperor Rudolph II who was surrounded by legends and whose fate is so closely connected to that of the Prague Castle. Three stone coats of arms are fixed beneath the window: to the left, the two tailed Bohemian lion, in the centre the flame eagle of St Wenceslas (the Bohemian heraldic beast of older times) and to the right the archbishop's coat of arms. From the two dials, with just one hand each, one can read the time: the topmost dial shows the hours and the lower dial the minutes and quarters of an hour.

Adjacent to the belfry is the world famous Golden Gate (Porta aurea) leading to the Cathedral's interior. A glass mosaic created by the Venetian craftsmen at the instruction of Emperor Charles IV sparkles in 30 different colours over three pointed arches. The mosaic reminds the beholder of the Last Judgement and the blazing flames of purgatory.

1

1 The interior offers the visitor an impressive panorama of the Gothic cathedral; the neo-Gothic construction in the area of the **nave** passes over almost seamlessly into the medieval section of the choir bathed in warm light.

2 **St Vitus Cathedral** at night (choir with chapels).

2

1 **St George's Basilica** from the tower of St Vitus Cathedral.

2 The basilica opens into the **Jiřská Lane** through an early Renaissance portal from the beginning of the 16th century, once again there is a depiction of St George battling the dragon in the portal's tympanum.

The foundation walls of the **St George's Basilica** originate from the 12th century, the brick-red façade from behind which the Romanesque choir towers rise up is however early Baroque. St George the dragon slayer stands guard in the tympanum at the front while on the portal ledge of the chapel built at the beginning of the 18th century, a statue of St Nepomuk looks down at the visitors. The Přemyslid tombs are to be found in the nave of this Romanesque church interior with the wooden beam ceiling. The founder of this church Vratislav I, deceased in 921 is buried here in a striking tomb. The painted Choir Chapel of St Ludmila is very important because of the grave of St Wenceslas grandmother. The stone figure on the tomb reminds of St Ludmila's martyrdom; she was attacked in her widow's home Tetín not far from Prague and was strangled with her veil 925 AD.

1 + 2   The **Golden Lane** at Prague Castle.

The medieval fortified wall of the ditch of the Brusnice stream behind the Castle created the architectonic basis for a small picturesque street, the **Goldmakers Lane**. Goldsmiths probably lived in the dwellings built beneath the fortified wall in the 15th century hence the name "Goldsmith Lane". The wretched huts and houses were demolished under Rudolph II; as a result the Emperor permitted 24 members of the castle guard to use the blind arcades beneath the battlemented parapet as storerooms.

2

Over the battlemented parapet whose crenelles enabled defending the Castle from the north in the 15th century, one reaches the so-called "White Tower", an artillery tower at the west end of the **Goldmakers Lane**. During the rule of Emperor Rudolph II this tower was a dark dungeon; on the ground floor above the dungeons was a torture chamber.

Kafka's little house in Golden Lane (no 22):
The probably best known resident of the Golden Lane was Franz Kafka who quartered himself in house no 22 for several months in 1916/17, and amongst others, wrote the narrations of the book *A Country Doctor*. A small bookshop has been set up here in his honour.

Towers of the stronghold fortification: **Daliborka** and **Black Tower**.

The **Old Castle stairway** connects the Castle to the Lesser Town.

Roof and chimney confusion in the **Lesser Town**.

THE LESSER TOWN

The narrow lanes, squares and gardens of this picturesque part of the city lie at the foot of two dominant hills: the Castle Hill with the Prague Castle borders the Lesser Town on the north, the wooded Petřín Hill forms the boundary on the south end.

The first signs of settlement in the Lesser Town in the area of the Bridge Lane [Mostecká] and Lesser Town Square [Malostranské náměstí] go back to the first century. Přemysl Otakar II finally established the Lesser Town in 1257, had it fortified and the wall built around it. Under the rule of Charles V, this part of the city was extended considerably on the south end to Petřín Hill and enclosed by the Hunger Wall built about 1360.

The Lesser Town was devastated during the Hussite wars because it posed as a strategic perimeter for the defence of the castle. The contending sides purposefully destroyed the buildings so that the enemy could not find cover. After the Hussites took over the Prague Castle on 7th July 1421, this part of the city was nothing but an expanse of rubble. The ruins of the Lesser Town of Prague could only be rebuilt and repaired by the extremely decimated citizenry many years later.

When King Vladislav Jagiello moved the royal seat from the Old Town to the Castle again in 1484, the Lesser Town was once again threatened due to its function as a strategic perimeter. But not only were armed conflicts to be feared; on the afternoon of 2nd June 1541 a fire broke out at the Lesser Town Square rapidly engulfing areas around it and soon developed into the most devastating conflagration in the history of Prague. This fire disaster entirely changed the appearance of the Lesser Town. The fire ruins were rebuilt in the then reigning Renaissance styles and even the buildings spared by the fire were remodelled according to contemporary taste.

Under the Habsburg crown and especially after the Battle of the White Mountain, the Lesser Town took on an increasingly feudal character. Many unfortunate Protestant noble families had to leave the town but Catholic aristocrats replaced them and settled down primarily in the immediate vicinity of the Imperial Castle. They built mansions and palaces in the Lesser Town and fulfilled their expectations of a representative lifestyle in the quiet lanes.

After the misery of the Thirty Years' War, new times had dawned when awareness of life is reflected in the opulent Baroque shapes too. Within one single generation emerged dozens of building and art monuments and this period moulded the appearance of the Lesser Town like no other to this day.

The Sala terrena of the **Waldstein Palace**.

One of the largest building projects in the Lesser Town was the **palace** of the Imperial Generalissimo **Albrecht of Waldstein**. Towards the garden is the architectonically significant Sala terrena decorated with frescoes. The replica of the bronze statues by Adrian de Vries have found an almost ideal installation spot to replace the originals that were transported by the Swedish troops to their homeland during the Thirty Years' War.

The **Lesser Town** transformed itself into a sleepy
area of town spared by
the hustle and bustle of
the 19th century and the
quiet spell prevails here
even today.

A look at the wintry **Lesser Town** (to the right, the towers of **St Nicholas**, left **St Thomas**).

On the southern side **Lobkowicz Palace** merges with the garden towards Petřín Hill.

1 The **Mácha Monument** on the Petřín Hill.   2 **St Lawrence Church** on the Petřín Hill.

With a height of 322 m the **Petřín Hill** is a moderate height for day trips, an ascending hillock on the left embankment in immediate neighbourhood of the Castle Hill. On the crest of Petřín Hill are a few objects of interest – an observatory, a mirror maze, the St Lawrence Church, rose gardens and a row of statues in honour of commendable personalities.

2

1 Viev of the **Lesser Town**, in the background (centre) **Strahov Monastery**.

2 Long before the people of Prague characterised their houses with numbers, they differentiated their buildings from each other by the so-called **house symbols**. The house symbols mostly have a connection, though often not relevant today, with the history of the house or the trade practiced. Many of these minor works of art that have been lovingly tended to can be seen especially along the Royal Path, in Nerudova Street in the Lesser Town.

Lesser Town Square from St Nicholas Church belfry.

The **Lesser Town City Hall** was the seat of the Lesser Town self-government.

The originally Protestant church of **Our Lady of Victory** of the Lesser Town Germans got its present name after the Battle of the White Mountain.

On a side-altar to the right is the gracious Prague Infant Jesus. The wax figure dressed in valuable robes originating from Spain in the 16th century is attributed with miraculous powers.

Lesser Town bridge towers, in front of it on the left, the former customs office: The smaller of the two towers originates from the same time as the Judith Bridge, the first stone bridge built over the Vltava. The tower is considered among the oldest structures in this town. The larger late Gothic tower was erected only in 1464. It was meant as a counterpart to the Old Town bridge towers.

With its impressive dome and the 79 m high belfry, the **St Nicholas Church** rises in the centre of the Lesser Town Square. This church is the most significant creation of high Baroque in Prague and was built between 1673 and 1755 on behalf of the Jesuits. The ceiling panel in the nave painted on an area of 1,500 m² is one of the largest frescoes in Europe.

The only Gothic church **St Thomas** originally built for the Benedictine monks was badly affected during the Hussite wars. Kilian Ignaz Dientzenhofer had the church remodelled in Baroque style between 1723 and 1731 and bestowed upon it the present appearance. The monastery was in the hands of the Augustine hermits since 1285.

Kampa Island, accessible from the Lesser Town (as well as from the Charles Bridge) lies between the River Vltava and the river arm "Devils Stream" [Čertovka]. Despite its location, the Kampa region came under the Old Town jurisdiction. Kampa Island was a storage place for trading commodities in the Middle Ages; in the course of centuries poor people mostly washerwomen and raftsmen settled down in this area that was subject to floods. Today Kampa Island is a tourism-oriented area with a smalltown character. It drifts over into a lively park in the southern part.

A particularly attractive part of the Kampa Island is known as "Venice of Prague" due to the buildings situated right by the water. A famous pottery market was held on the island for centuries.

PRAGUE UNDER WATER

On 12th August 2002, an unexpected tidal wave reaches the city of Prague. Karlín, Libeň, the Lesser Town – within a few hours, entire areas are engulfed in the murky floods, people and animals succumb to the flood, irreplaceable valuables and cultural possessions are destroyed. Prague residents – and with them, millions of people all over the world – wait with bated breath; Prague is under water. Tens of thousands of people are evacuated during the flood, thousands of flood helpers – police, soldiers and civil-

A look at the worst affected **Lesser Town**.

ians – are brought into operation. Historic buildings are endangered, the first buildings collapse. Apart from the tremendous material damages in the entire country, estimated at about 100 billion crowns, there are irreplaceable damages to cultural heritage in the City Centre; the National Theatre, Rudolfinum, the Jewish Museum, several theatres and also private cultural institutions report severe damages. It takes almost a week until the water ebbs away and clearing up action progresses up, but the affected areas of the city bear a ghostly resemblance for months to come.

Even **Franz Kafka** can hardly keep his head above water.

CHARLES BRIDGE

Thanks to Smetana's symphonic poetry, the Vltava is perhaps one of the best known rivers in the world, although by world standard it is more a humble rivulet: the 31 km flowing through Prague have an average depth of about 4 m. Nonetheless, it is sufficient to ply all kinds of vehicles on: excursion ships cruise past the world famous sights, chug towards Roztoky or to the Prague Zoo and reach the Slapy Dam, the last large weir of the Vltava before Prague, in a span of only four hours from the City Centre. Humble though this rivulet might be, the Prague Steamship Company makes a livelihood plying its trade under 17 Prague bridges.

The Gothic Charles Bridge is considered as one of the most important monuments of medieval architecture in Bohemia. As early as the 9th century there is believed to have been a ferry here that was, as the well-known Bohemian chronicler Cosmas informs us, substituted by a wooden bridge latest by 1118. The first stone bridge replaced the wooden construction in 1158. This firmly established Judith Bridge served the Prague residents for almost two centuries until it was swept away by the floods in 1342. At exactly the time predicted by the court astrologers – in the year 1357, on the 9th day of the 7th month, at 5:31 h – Emperor Charles IV laid the foundation for the construction of the new bridge that would stretch over the Vltava with sixteen arches and be about 5 m higher than its predecessor. The architect and master builder Peter Parler came from Schwäbisch Gmünd. The stone bridge remains the only connection between the Old Town of Prague and the Lesser Town until into the 19th century. Of the 30 sculptures on the Charles Bridge, mostly replaced by copies today, the one of St Nepomuk is the most important. It was cast in 1683 based on a model by Johann Brokoff in Nuremberg. Anybody wanting to enjoy the port atmosphere, ought to stroll below the embankment to the jetty once and admire the colourful activity and port life that has developed there; restaurant ships and so-called botels are anchored here, small cafés on the riverbanks beckon, travel agents on the lookout for clients, freshwater sailors and tourist guides wait for the next excursion ship to dock. Here too, we are welcomed by the lovely greeting "Ahoj!" again and again – there is no doubt any more: Bohemia lies near the sea.

The Prague cityscape is shaped considerably by the Vltava: Altogether 17 bridges stretch over the river, the oldest and best known of them is the **Charles Bridge**.

Early morning on the **Charles Bridge**,
the bronze statue of St Nepomuk to the left.

1 Almost 300 years after his martyrdom in 1683, the bronze statue of **St Nepomuk** made by Johann Brokoff was installed on the Charles Bridge. King Wenceslas IV had him thrown into the tide from the stone bridge over the River Vltava. The legend goes that he did not wish to divulge the pious Queen Sophie's confessional secret as demanded by the cruel king n hence he had to forfeit his life.

2 The **government building** directly at the riverside not far from the Mánes Bridge.

The **Charles Bridge** made of stone.

THE OLD TOWN

Embedded in the riverbend, with the river flowing around it in a semicircle and therefore ideally protected is the location of the first of the four historical cities of Prague: the Old Town of Prague. Its beginnings go back to the first century of the Christian calendar – there was obviously no reason to name the small market town Old Town at that time. This term came to be used only after Charles IV founded the "New Town" in the 14th century. The Prague Jewish Town developed in the northwest of the Old Town area bordering directly on the banks of the River Vltava. The centre of the Old Town consists of the Old Town Square with its dominant City Hall and Týn Church. Another significant city-core developed around the St Gallus Church: the Gallus Town. In the course of the administrative reform under Emperor Joseph II, the Prague towns namely Castle District, the Lesser Town, New Town and Old Town united in 1784. From then onwards, the City Hall of Prague was located at the Old Town Square.

In the 20th century the Old Town of Prague underwent some drastic changes that have robbed the area of a lot of its former charm. The redevelopment of the Prague Jewish Quarter (about 1900) can be cited as an example, the politically driven removal of the Marian column that used to be in front of the City Hall (1918) and the destruction of the east wing of the neo-Gothic City Hall during the Prague rebellions in May 1945. Despite many losses the Old Town of Prague is counted amongst the most beautiful historical ensemble of Europe today.

With the construction of the Charles Bridge in 1357, Peter Parler also began building the Gothic defence tower on the Old Town bridgehead. This tower was of great strategic significance in defending the Old Town (like against the Swedes in the Thirty Years' War). Fortunately this bulwark survived the violent centuries relatively undamaged. Only the ornamental figures on the west side were destroyed and removed during the Swedish shooting raid in 1648. An old inscription commemorates it.

To the east of the tower, above the pointed archway, the coat of arms of countries that were reigned by Charles IV can be seen. Beneath the coat of arms is portrayed the kingfisher, symbol of King Wenceslas IV. Above the row of coat of arms stands St Vitus as the bridge protector on three bridge piers flanked by the two patrons: Charles IV (left) and Wenceslas IV (right). On the top floor of the tower are the saints Adalbert and Sigismund above the (Bohemian) lion sculpture inset in the façade.

One can climb up to the tower gallery through a spiral staircase and enjoy the view over the rooftops of the Old Town.

1 A **statue of Emperor Charles IV** dominates the Knights of the Cross Square.

2 The monastery church of **the Order of the Knights of the Cross St Franciscus Seraphicus** of the greatly esteemed and the sole one of the order of the knights founded in Bohemia, the "Knights of the Cross with a Red Star" is a replica of the St Peter's Cathedral in Rome and like its model impresses first and foremost with its magnificent dome.

The **Old Town Square:** The important monuments, palaces and churches are joined by proud middle-class buildings with individual history going back into the Middle Ages.

Gothic, Renaissance and Baroque united into a unique composition that is rightly perceived as the **centre** of the historical cities of Prague.

The **Jan Hus Monument** at the **Old Town Square**.

The **Jan Hus Monument** by Ladislav Ša-loun, too large as compared to the extent of the square was unveiled on 6th July 1915 on the 500th anniversary of the reformer Jan Hus' burning to death. The upright Hus looks at the Týn Church that was the Hussite Bishop's Church for a while.

The church **"Our Lady before Týn"** was founded by traders and merchants in the mid 14th century. The construction work was done by Peter Parler's cathedral stonemasonry. The 80 m high towers with eight pointed spires each is a characteristic landmark in the maze of roofs in the Old Town.

The arcade like porch that restricts the view of the church housed the "Týn School" even in the Middle Ages. In the church interior is the marble tomb of the important Danish

Towers of the **Týn Church**.

astronomer Tycho de Brahe. Emperor Rudolph II summoned him to Prague in 1599. The life-size relief figure is dressed in full armour.

The construction was stopped during the Hussite unrests. The elected King George of Poděbrady had the church and the two distinctive towers on it completed. A statue of George of Poděbrady with a drawn sword portrayed as the protector of the Hussite chalice was placed on the gable roof. It was removed soon after the victory of the Catholic Habsburgs at the Battle of the White Mountain and the gilded chalice was thereafter melted into the halo for the predominant Madonna statue on the gable roof.

Since the Middle Ages, the pillory and the place of execution were placed in front of the **Old Town City Hall**.

The **Apostle Clock** is a mirror of the medieval view of the world: The planets are depicted circling the earth not the sun.

[1] The building **"At the Minute"** has a sgraffito façade from the beginning of the 17th century. The guarding lion on the building corner is the trademark of the former pharmacy "At the White Lion" situated here.

[2] The **Kinsky Palace** (left) is a mature later work of Kilian Ignaz Dientzenhofer. The three-storeyed tower building **"At the Stone Bell"** (right) was built on the foundations of an early Gothic residential building in the second half of 13th century.

1 The splendid Baroque Church **St Nicholas in the Old Town** was built in 1732–1737 in the immediate neighbourhood of the Jewish Quarter. It is the work of the famous Kilian Ignaz Dientzenhofer.

2 In the church interior is an admirably splendid **chandelier** from the bohemian town in the Giant
Mountains, Harrachov and a large fresco with a legend of St Nicholas as the theme.

1   **Karlova Lane**, the connecting lane between the Charles Bridge and the Old Town Square described as "Jesuits Lane" in its time is now one of Prague's liveliest lanes.

2   The premiere of important operas were held in the **Estates Theatre**, for example Mozart's *Don Giovanni* (1787) and *La clemenza di Tito* (1791).

THE JEWISH QUARTER

No one can say for certain when the Jews came to Bohemia, where and in what numbers they settled down. The beginnings lie in darkness.

From written sources of the early Middle Ages it is evident that Jewish traders, physicians and civil servants lived in Prague. At least two Jewish settlements can be proved to have existed in the 10th and 11th centuries, one below the Prague Castle and another at Vyšehrad. After 1100 the Jewish community settled in the area of the Spanish Synagogue. The widely known Prague Jewish Town, the walled ghetto in the Old Town finally developed itself towards the end of the 12th century.

Prague Jewry experienced its heyday under the rule of Rudolph II when Mordechai Maisel, the mayor of the Jewish Town and the Emperor's court financier blessed with earthly goods, had the ghetto lanes paved, provided for deserted brides, had synagogues, schools, baths and the famous City Hall built and of course the Jewish Cemetery "Beth-Chaim" (House of Life) laid out. The esteemed Rabbi Loew worked and taught in the Prague Jewish Town around the same time – not only was he to go down in history as an important cabbalist and theologist but also as the creator of the Golem – at the centre of many legends. This creation of Rabbi Loew, so the legend goes, stood on their side as an emergency helper in times of persecution. The entire Jewry was driven out of its inherited hometown twice: 1541 under the rule of Emperor Ferdinand I and 1744 under Maria Theresa's rule, who ordered by decree the expulsion of all Jews from Bohemia. Three years after the last families had left their homes, the monarch found herself forced to revoke the expulsion decree. Only with the issue of the toleration edict by her son Joseph II did the situation change fundamentally for the Jews. The Jewish Town which is now called Josefov in his honour however fell into disrepair due to the moving away of affluent families to posher parts of the city. Evil dives, poverty and prostitution soon characterised the appearance of Josefov. After several meetings and decisions a seminal cleanup was implemented about 1890, unfortunately a large part of the historical fabric was also ruined in the process. In place of the twisty dark lanes of the poor came the modern art nouveau palaces of rich citizens and industrialists. The national socialist rulers eventually dealt the death blow to the Jewish community. Almost 80,000 Jews from the Reich Protectorate Bohemia-Moravia lost their lives in the occupation years between 1939 and 1945.

1 The characteristic brick gable of the **Old-New Synagogue** was added on to the existing building only in the 15th century. This temple is the oldest synagogue in Europe still serving its purpose.

2 The **Jewish City Hall** built by the Italian architect Pankraz Roder in the 1680s is situated in close proximity of the Old-New Synagogue. Two clocks adorned the tower, one with the Latin and the other with Hebrew numbers that go from right to the left like the Hebrew script.

1. The **Spanish Synagogue** is made as a reproduction of the Spanish Alhambra. The gilded stucco-work interior and the Moorish appearance of the temple was intended to commemorate the Jews driven out of Spain who had found refuge in Prague for a while.

2. A **monument for Franz Kafka** was unveiled in close proximity of the Spanish Synagogue in December 2003. The bronze statue by the Czech sculptor Jaroslav Rona shows the poet "riding" on the shoulders of a headless male figure.

1

The members of the Czechoslovakian National Assembly debated in this building in the years 1918–1939, now the **Rudolfinum** serves the muses again under the name "House of Artists". Regular concerts including the Czech Philharmonic Orchestra are organised here and the famous music festival "Prague Spring" has found a home here.

"In the **ditch**" [Na Příkopě].

THE NEW TOWN

The New Town established more than 650 years ago by Charles IV in 1348 in place of older settlements can hardly do its name justice. Of course it is virginal as compared to the Old Town or the Prague Castle – the beginnings of which go back to the first century AD.

With the founding of the New Town, Emperor Charles IV gave the city Prague, bursting at the seams, further scope for development. He not only divided the course of the streets and squares but also dictated the location of the churches that were to be made of stone. The medieval regional development and traffic planning sufficed for the technical demands into the 20th century.

The New Town has in a way maintained a very youthful and lively atmosphere even today. Life in the capital is happening here, important business houses have their branches here and this is where the great political and cultural manifestations and revolutions took place especially in the 20th century. The Czechoslovakian Republic was proclaimed at the Wenceslas Square, sloping upwards to the National Museum, on 28th October 1918. The masses gathered here in 1945, 1968 and 1989 partly in order to watch, partly to push ahead the respective political changes.

The Wenceslas square extends from Můstek at the border of the Old Town up to the Horse Gate that was situated where the National Museum is today. At the beginning of the 19th century the largest boulevard of Prague (750 x 60 m) was still surrounded by one to three-storey buildings, it took on the character of a capital city only in the 20th century. On the broad pavements of the shopping street flanked by limetree avenues, the young Prague meets tourists from all over the world. The judgement of the German poet Detlev von Liliencron who termed Wenceslas Square the "World's proudest boulevard" is true even today. It was also known as "Horse Market" until 1848 because of the equestrian markets held here annually. The Czech journalist and author Karel Havlíček Borovský suggested renaming of the boulevard to its present name Wenceslas Square in the revolution year 1848.

In 1912 a statue of the Bohemian national patron St Wenceslas on horseback was placed at Wenceslas Square. A series of memorable events of the national political history are closely connected with the statue. The Prague people in contrast are fond of "their horse" because the place "under the tail" is wellknown as the venue for the gallant dates and lovers rendezvous. Even "babička" (grandma) stood here in her young years with a throbbing heart … certainly not pondering over politics!

Chic and elegance dominate the expensive and posh New Town with its central **Wenceslas Square**.

Wenceslas Square with the **National Museum** at night.

The **central station** originally named after Emperor Francis Joseph was built in 1901–1909 based on the plans of Josef Fanta. The four stone towers in the Prague Secession style lend it a distinctive appearance.

1 The **National Theatre** with room for more than 1,800 spectators built exclusively from local building material belongs to the most magnificent neo-Renaissance constructions in Prague.

2 The **Dancing House:** The two cylindrical structures of the building jokingly called Ginger Rogers and Fred Astaire contrast with the surrounding almost uniform turn-of-the-century architecture.

1

THE OUTSKIRTS

The citadel **Vyšehrad**, a Baroque fortification lies calm and mysterious on a rocky ledge high above the Vltava embankment. It is presumed that here, to the south of Prague there already existed an old Slavic castle in the eighth century, the first written mention though is in the chronicles from the year 1002. In the course of the century long history, Vyšehrad was the royal seat, a small market town, Bohemia's religious centre, Baroque fortress and outing destination for the capital's residents.

Villa Bertramka is a small former vineyard in Smíchov, a suburb outside the city walls. Mozart was a guest of his Prague friends František and Josepha Dušek in the idyllic country house in 1787. His opera *Don Giovanni* that held its premier performance in the Estates Theatre is believed to have been completed in the Villa Bertramka.

Archduke Ferdinand of Tyrol had the **Summer Residence Hvĕzda** (Czech word for star) built in the Renaissance style in 1555. He chose to give it the shape of a six-radial star.

The historical Battle of the White Mountain where the Protestant Bohemian estates were defeated by the Catholic league was fought on grounds nearby.

The **Summer Residence Troja**, one of the magnificent palaces in the country and at the same time a masterpiece of Bohemian Baroque was built in the years 1680–1688 for Count Wenzel Adalbert of Sternberg. The Troja Chateau has a uniquely beautiful open stairway with figures from the Greek mythology.

Nature lovers can not only visit the Pomological Institute (Institute for fruit-growing) but also the Prague Zoo as well as the Orchard [Stromovka] one of the most attractive garden complexes in Central Europe.

110

110

1 The **Benedictine abbey Břevnov** is the oldest monastery in Prague and at the same time the starting point for many subsidiaries in the country. The present monastery church was erected at the beginning of the 18th century by Christoph Dientzenhofer.

2 The **television tower** in Žižkov (futurism).